A Brief History of Tim

A BRIEF HISTORY OF TIM

The World Minus One Letter

Kathy Clugston

2 4 6 8 10 9 7 5 3 1

Published in 2010 by Virgin Books, an imprint of Ebury Publishing

A Random House Group Company

Copyright © Kathy Clugston 2010

Illustrations Copyright © Tom McLaughlin 2010

Designed by Lindsay Nash

Kathy Clugston has asserted her right under the Copyright, Designs and Patents Act 1988 to be identified as the author of this work

The Random House Group Limited Reg. No. 954009

Addresses for companies within the Random House Group can be found at www.randomhouse.co.uk

A CIP catalogue record for this book is available from the British Library

The Random House Group Limited supports The Forest Stewardship Council [FSC], the leading international forest certification organisation. All our titles that are printed on Greenpeace-approved FSC-certified paper carry the FSC logo. Our paper procurement policy can be found at www.rbooks.co.uk/environment

Mixed Sources
Product group from well-managed forests and other controlled sources
www.fsc.org Cert no. TT-COC-2139
FSC © 1996 Forest Stewardship Council

Printed and bound in Great Britain by CPI Mackays, Chatham ME5 8TD

ISBN 9780753522684

To buy books by your favourite authors and register for offers visit www.rbooks.co.uk

For Mum and Mac, with love.

—Magnifique

Contents

A Brief History of Tim

An Explanation

Late one night, alone on a train from Heathrow airport, I was thinking about the long-running Radio 4 programme *Gardeners' Question Time* (well, you do, don't you?) when I knocked a letter off the end and got **Gardeners' Question Tim** (outdoor dilemmas solved by someone called Tim). Then came **Boo of the Week** (a scary story). I posted them on Twitter and the response was brilliant: in the short time it took me to get home there were dozens of replies, such as **I'm Sorry I Haven't a Cue** (the antidote to snooker games), and **Rain of Britain** (the weather forecast), which had me snorting loudly on the train and getting looks from my fellow passengers.

Silly word games like this have been around for ever – or at least since the day some wag made 'alpha' and 'beta' into 'alphabet' – and to judge by Twitter alone, which is regularly awash with clever plays on song, TV and film titles, they never tire.

Two days later, there were over 2,000 #radio4minus1letter tweets and I was invited on to Radio 4's *Broadcasting House* to explain the game, resulting in yet more brilliant ideas from listeners. I began to think more about this gardening expert Tim and the world in which he might live, a world where everything – books, TV programmes, films, places, events, even history – had a letter missing: just one letter taken away, no letters added or switched, and no misspellings. And so *A Brief History of Tim* was born.

I really hope you enjoy it. It shouldn't take too long to read; you know how **Tim flies**.

Kathy

PS I've included a Radio 4 section (in the TV and Radio chapter) in honour of the original game. Although many of the early suggestions have long since vanished into the ether, I remembered tons of them. So thank you, tweeters and *BH* listeners, for letting me shamelessly, er, borrow your ideas.

1. History

A Brief History of the World

The Big Bag
Where all the particles are kept before they accidentally spill out and create the universe.

65 million years BC

All the dinosaurs become **Tyrannosaurus ex**. No one knows exactly why they died out; one theory is that they suddenly became vain and aggressive with overdeveloped muscles that made it difficult to hunt. This is known as the **steroid theory**.

2 million years BC

Humans stop monkeying around and
learn to sing in the period known as the
tone age.

3000 years BC

The ancient kingdom of Egypt builds up around the **River Nil**. Once baby Moses is fished out of his basket, nothing much else happens.

2000 years BC

The ancient Geeks

Nerdy types who spend far too much time doing maths. They worship many deities, including the god of detection, **Hercule**, and the god of having the weight of the world on your shoulders, **Alas**. Later, the ancient Romans have similar gods, such as **Mar**, the god of ruin, and **A Polo**, the god of fresh breath.

1500 years BC

The cast system evolves in India. Some people get much better parts than others.

The Ha! Dynasty

The ancient Chinese invent paper, ink and porcelain – take that, rest of the world!

The Chinese are also the first to shout loudly at fire, thereby inventing the **bellow**, and indeed they are responsible for many more useful things: **oodles**, in fact.

Three Other Notable Chinese Dynastic Discoveries

The Mig Dynasty:
The jet fighter plane.

The Tan Dynasty:
The sun lamp.

The Chin Dynasty:
Bruce Forsyth.

AD 731

An exhausted Anglo-Saxon monk finally completes his written history of the Church of England and takes to his **Venerable Bed**.

1066

The Battle of Hatings

William I and King Harold do not see eye to eye.

Ow!
How very pointed!

1160

King Arthur, eager for a new quest, holds a mammoth brain-storming session and after **twelve nights of the round-table** discussions, decides to find the hallowed object on which Jesus hung his coat during the Last Supper, the **Holy Rail**.

1314

After burning the cakes, Robert the Bruce redeems himself with a tasty victory at the **Battle of Bannock Bun**.

1492

Christopher Columbus sails the wrong way to Asia but discovers a **new word**. That word is 'America'. The indigenous peoples welcome the disease-ridden settlers with open arms, and are therefore known as **Naive Americans**.

1666

The Great Fir of London: a dodgy set of Christmas lights on Norway's traditional Yuletide gift results in tragedy.

1770

Captain Coo finds Australia and goes all soppy over it.

1837

Queen Victoria ascends the British throne. She allows her husband, Prince Albert, an unusual amount of freedom, keeping him on the **longest rein in British history**.

1845

The start of the devastating potato famine in Ireland. It has since been revealed that the potato is a staple food for humans because we share an astonishing 95 per cent of our DNA with **chips**.

1865

The 13th Amendment to the American Constitution bans the nefarious practices of drooling, dribbling and slobbering. At long last, **slaver** is abolished.

1912

The *Titanic* is unexpectedly painted. It had previously been thought **uninkable**.

The Modern Age

1920s

The first **Marie Stops clinics** advocate complete abstinence from sex. It wasn't until the 1960s that the headache was invented and became the first type of **contraceptive ill**.

With great regret, **Home Rue** is introduced in Ireland.

Catastrophe strikes the hosiery industry in the great **Sock Market Crash**.

1930s

A useful guide to all the public baths in London is published. The **tub map** becomes a design classic.

Pointy-headed **Arrow Marchers** fly straight to Westminster to protest at the government's failure to reach employment targets.

The England cricket team categorically deny bowling straight at Don Bradman in the **Body Lie** series.

1940s

The forties are dominated by the Second World War years, otherwise known as **era Lynn**.

Woody Guthrie strikes a blow for paternity rights campaigners everywhere with his song **This Lad Is Your Lad**.

The **National Heath Service** is founded, allowing free access to coarse grassland for all.

1950s

In Europe, a highly charged electric fence, the **Ion Curtain** continues to separate East and West.

The dramatic decline in the number of baby girls being named Susan leads to the **Sue Crisis**.

Efforts are made to introduce standard, cheap writing implements across Europe through the **Euro Pen Economic Community**.

1960s

The extremely short comedy sketch, the **mini-skit**, becomes fashionable.

Martin Luther King makes the longest speech in history. It uses a record number of sheets of paper and becomes known as **'I Have a Ream'**.

The beginning of the space race. Everyone is amazed when a horse exits the earth's atmosphere on the first **maned mission to the moon**.

1970s

The world's first **Tet-tube baby** is born in Vietnam.

Reducing energy consumption is not a new idea – back in the early seventies, hippies were very ecologically minded and advocated **lower power**.

Britain and Iceland angle for the rights to a brand new music format in a series of **CD wars**.

1980s

The **Falk Land war**. There's an unexpectedly violent reaction to the BBC cancelling *Columbo*.

Margaret Thatcher has coaching to lower the pitch of her voice, despite having defiantly told the electorate **'the lady's not for tuning'**.

Pop stars give their flagging careers a boost by appearing in the **Band Ad** video.

1990s

Endangered aquatic mammals in Britain start to be supported by the **National Ottery**.

Bill Clinton admits that his affair with Monica Lewinsky gave him no pleasure whatsoever, announcing: 'I did not have **sexual elations** with that woman.'

Genetic scientists reveal the shape of things to come as Dolly the Sheep is **coned**.

2000s

Politicians from all sides in Northern Ireland start running their own parliament in a process known as **evolution**.

President Obama takes over from President Bush and declares the **War on Error** a big mistake.

This decade was nicknamed the **oughties** because we really should have seen the credit crunch coming. There is much discussion about who is responsible for it all, and in particular the level of **bank onuses**.

2. TV and Radio

The world's first broadcasting organisation was created in Britain in 1922. It had only one employee, a radio announcer called Bradley, and was accordingly named the **British Brad Casting Company**. When it expanded and became a corporation, no one minded in the least, this being the **ireless** age.

Television followed in the 1930s, but it wasn't until the fifties that it became common to have a TV in the home. The demand for televisions soared after 1953, when millions of people gathered around the nearest set to watch Princess Elizabeth have a **crow** placed on her head and take the **coronation oat**. Sales of muesli also rocketed.

Early television programmes for children often involved puppets, such as **Torchy the Batter Boy**, who was transported to a faraway star to make pancakes. Kids also loved the short films between programmes, a favourite being **The Potter's Heel** in which a man sloughed the hard skin off his feet. **Watch Wit, Mother!** was a popular strand of children's programmes with an insidious reminder to women that it was unwise in these pre-feminist times to exhibit a sense of humour.

As new TV channels came along, adults could enjoy hard-hitting drama like **Arm Hair Theatre**, which dealt with issues of social depilation, and entertainment programmes such as **This is Your Lie**, where famous guests talked us through their fascinating, virtuous, celebrity-filled lives. These days, two popular favourites are **Coe, Dine with Me**, where a group of strangers try to persuade Lord Sebastian Coe to come round for dinner, and **Strictly Coe Dancing**, where Lord Sebastian Coe performs a variety of ballroom and Latin routines entirely on his own.

Vintage Radio Classics

Dick Baron
Daily adventures of the nobleman special agent.

The Go On, How?
Spike Milligan, Peter Sellers and Michael Bentine explain how things work in funny, high-pitched voices.

Take it from Her
Rather one-sided divorce advice.

Workers' Pay Time
Live salary disputes from various locations across the country.

TV Comedy

Auf Wiedersehen ET

A bunch of unemployed brickies find work
three million light years from home.

The Fat Show
Comedy sketch programme with a lot of
padding.

Fawlty Owers
Classic comedy set in a chaotic Torquay bank.

Genus
Dave Gorman asks members of the public to
come up with hilarious new taxonomic
classifications.

The Hick of It
Scathing satire about a country bumpkin who
becomes a cabinet minister.

Inner Ladies
Victoria Wood's comedy about a group of
transvestites in Manchester.

I Sing Damp

A parsimonious landlord annoys his
tenants by belting out xenophobic
songs in the shower.

The Liver Bids

Reality show in which the public vote to decide
which of a pair of fun-loving flatmates in
Liverpool is the most deserving transplant
patient.

The Mighty Boos

A pair of oddly dressed comedians are loudly
heckled.

On the Uses

Travelling DIY show.

One Foot in the Rave

Grumpy old man does the hokey-cokey
on ecstasy.

The Ood Life

Felicity Kendal and Richard Briers pursue an alternative lifestyle as squid-faced humanoids.

Pep Show

Motivational comedy from Mitchell and Webb.

teams, those are no ordinary buzzers...

Q

Stephen Fry's Bond-themed panel game.

TV and Radio Comedians

Itch Benn
Keen.

Alan Car
Racy.

Jack De and Stewart Le
Both aspire to be Dawn French.

Richard Erring
Wrong.

Jeremy Hard
Tough.

Miranda Hat
Warm.

Josie Log
Has to write everything down.

Avid Mitchell and Robert Ebb
One is very keen, the other is slightly
losing interest.

Victoria Woo
Knows how to get the audience on her
side. Had to get rid of her comedy
partner **Julie Alters** when she started
changing everything.

The Smoking Roo
Australian version of *Pets Do the Funniest Things*.

Yes, Minster
Satire about the political machinations at the highest level of the Church of England.

TV Drama and Factual

Ales of the Unexpected
Roald Dahl finds cherry beer surprisingly palatable.

Amish Macbeth
The adventures of a Mennonite police constable in the Highlands.

Bakes 7

A band of renegade cooks rebel against a tyrannical head chef.

The Blue Plant

David Attenborough's stunning documentary series about a sad hydrangea.

Bookside

The lives and loves of a cul-de-sacful of literary Liverpudlians.

Casual T

It's dress-down Friday at Holby A&E.

Crown Curt

Courtroom drama in which the judges' verdicts are incredibly brusque.

The Cult RE Show
Weekly religious sect news.

Dr Ho
Long-running sci-fi series about a time-travelling Vietnamese revolutionary. **David Tenant** was one of the role's temporary residents.

Emergency Wad 10
Popular medical drama highlighting the plight of under-resourced staff, who have to use cotton wool for pretty much everything.

House of Cars
Greed, power and corruption in a second-hand motor dealership.

I'm a Gin
Arts programme in which Alan Yentob goes to the opera and orders his interval drink.

Inspector More

The classical-music-loving Oxford detective's appetite for solving crime is insatiable.

The Ire

The action in this tense and complex Baltimore police drama is fast and furious.

Jonathan Reek

Smelly magician solves mysteries.

Murder She Rote

Angela Lansbury unmasks killers with monotonous regularity.

News Nigh

Things are going to happen. Any minute now.

Pa! No Ram!

Hard-hitting reports about child farmers.

Prim Suspect

Helen Mirren tracks down a serial killer by following a trail of twinsets and sensible shoes.

The Scent of Man

Ground-breaking olfactory series, shown on the **BO** network in America.

The South Ban Show

Melvyn Bragg is barred from profiling any famous artistic figures who aren't from the north.

A Touch of Frot

Yorkshire detective solves crime by day and engages in furtive fumbling by night.

Twin Peas

Quirky David Lynch series about vegetables that look mysteriously alike.

The Ukes of Hazzard

Bo, Luke and Daisy Duke take up the ukulele.

Woking Lunch

Consumer programme in which Declan Curry investigates the price of sandwiches in Surrey.

TV Entertainment

Ash in the Attic

Hints and tips on raising money by setting fire to your home.

Children's Television through the Years

Bag Pus

The adventures of Emily and her old, saggy, cloth, disease-ridden cat.

Lay School
Educational series about what happens
when Mummy and Daddy want a
new carpet.

The Magi Roundabout
Animated Bible stories featuring the
Galilean fisherman Zebedee, who always
had a spring in his step.

Multi-Coloured Sap Shop
Kids' gardening phone-in from
the eighties.

Press Gag
Drama about a youth newspaper
in Zimbabwe.

Read Steady Go
Cool and trendy literacy programme.

Children's Television contd

Rent a Host
Children's version of *Have I Got News for You*.

The Soot Show
A puppet show so old it was first made for children who were sent up chimneys.

Top of the Ops
Aspiring young nurses and doctors were glued to this weekly countdown of the nation's favourite surgical procedures.

Bargain Hun

A guide to finding Attila memorabilia at knock-down prices.

Big Bother

Reality show that's really not worth switching over for.

Britain's Next to PM Ode

A selection of very thin girls compete for the chance to honour the incumbent of Number 10 in verse.

Count Dow

Daily afternoon coverage of the US stock market.

Dancing Nice

Celebrities are paired with professional ice skaters and banned from spitting, hair-pulling or telling tales.

Drag On Den

New inventions are demonstrated to potential investors. At length.

Gee!

Gosh, another American show about high-school kids.

Lockbusters

General knowledge quiz in which teenage housebreakers compete to win a dictionary.

Lose Women

Can someone please make them stop?

The On Show

Magazine programme that will definitely be going ahead tonight.

Rumpy Old Men

Oh look, they seem to have cheered up a bit.

Songs of Prise

Harry Secombe hums while taking the lid off a jam jar.

Top Ear

Souped-up version of *Name That Tune*.

The Weakest Ink

Is it any wonder Anne Robinson can't read her questions out properly?

The X Actor

Simon Cowell pretends to be amazed when someone unattractive/overweight/over 25 can actually sing.

BBC Radio 4

Where Tim was born – see pages 1–3 for an explanation

0520 **The Sipping Forecast**
Warm cup of tea moving slowly
southwards. Sugars 1 or 2. Toast later.
Good.

0530 **New Briefing**
A different format every day. Followed
by **Payer for the Day**, in which one of
the newsreaders volunteers to go and get
the cappuccinos.

0545 **Arming Today**
John Humphrys and co. prepare
themselves for those really tough
political interviews.

0600 **T'day**
Australian current affairs programme.

0900 **In Our Tie**
Melvyn Bragg and a distinguished panel discuss neckwear through the ages.

0945 **Book of the Wee**
Toilet book.

1000 **Woman's Hur**
Live coverage of female chariot racing.

1100 **From Our Own Co-Respondent**
News from the divorce courts.

1130 **Cross Incontinents**
Well, you would be, wouldn't you?

1200 **Yo! and Yours**
Long-running consumer programme
attempts to become more 'street'.

1300 **The Word at One**
Extremely short news programme.

1400 **The Achers**
Daily drama set in a retirement home.

1415 **The Afternoon Lay**
Time to switch off the radio and do
something more interesting.

1500 **Money Box Lie**
Interviews with bankers and stock-
market brokers.

1530 **Am I Norma?**
Mrs Major questions her very existence.

1600 **Thin Kin Allowed**
Social engineering programme that aims
to get rid of overweight relatives.

1625 **The Radio 4 Appal**
A short plea from a disgruntled listener.

1630 **A Good Red**
Sue MacGregor and her guests share
their favourite affordable wines.

1700 **P**
Eddie Mair takes a comfort break.

1800 **The Six Clock News**
Big Ben is replaced by a variety of
timepieces.

1830 **The No Show**
Thirty minutes of silence when the
comedians Steve Punt and Hugh Dennis
fail to turn up.

1900 **The Archer**
Only David is left as a deadly virus
sweeps through Ambridge.

1915 **Font Row**
Nightly argument about which typeface
is the best.

2000 **The Oral Maze**
Michael Buerk hosts a heated debate
about the intricacies of dentistry.

2100 **Fie on 4!**
Extracts from Shakespeare.

2200 **The Wold Tonight**
The latest news and analysis from Stow.

2245 **Bok at Bedtime**
Late-night tale read by a South African rugby player.

2300 **Cain Pressure**
Airborn comedy about two warring brothers.

2330 **Poetry Pleas**
Every week listeners beg for their favourite poems to be read out.

0000 **The Midnight Ews**
A round-up of the most disgusting stories of the day.

0030 **Boo of the Week**
Late-night scary story.

0040 **Ailing By**
Piece of instrumental music that limps
along.

Other radio stations are available:

Capita Radio
Every listener is an individual.

The Classic FM Most Waned
Listeners choose the pieces of music that have become gradually less impressive over the years.

Five Live Dive
Peter Allen and Anita Anand broadcast from a really grotty studio.

I Tune
Radio 3 programme in which we hear a famous musician warming up.

Pick of the Pop
Dale Winton chooses his favourite carbonated drinks, past and present, for Radio 2.

Planet Roc
The home of music legends.

The Scott Ills Show
Join Radio 1's favourite hypochondriac
for daily updates on his ailments.

Simon May
Or then again, he may not.

A Solute Radio
Has the right chemistry.

Sooth Radio
Speaks the truth.

talkPORT
Sophisticated after-dinner conversation.

For Your Weekend R4 Listening Pleasure

Anal Sis
Advice on what to do about overly tidy siblings.

Bell on Sunday
BBC cutbacks take their toll.

Broadcasting Hose
Weekly tights and stockings news.

Excess Bag Age
Sandi Toksvig throws out all her
old suitcases.

Loose End
Clive Anderson interviews anyone he
finds hanging around with nothing
better to do.

Po File
An in-depth look at a chamber pot
in the news.

3. Literature

Books

Pre-Twentieth-Century Classics

Far from the Madding Crow
The beautiful Bathsheba moves to Weatherbury to escape a really annoying bird.

Indication of the Rights of Women
The eighteenth-century feminist Mary Wollstonecraft points out a few home truths in her tome, a major work of the **Age of Enlighten Men**.

Lack Beauty
A sweet-natured black horse has a succession of owners, all of whom wish he was just a bit more attractive.

Lice in Wonderland
Alice's head begins to feel a little itchy.

Little Omen

Meg, Jo and Beth should have known something was amiss when baby Amy's first words were 'six, six, six'.

Madame Ovary

A French doctor's wife is possessed of an over-fertile imagination.

The Man in the Ron Mask

The evil King of France imprisons his twin brother in the Bastille and disguises him as Ron Atkinson so that no one will be able to understand him. The Three Musketeers hatch a plot to spring him early doors.

Middle Mach

When Dorothea's husband drops dead she rushes to the altar with his cousin at somewhere between supersonic and hypersonic speed.

Three Dickens Novels

Liver Twist
The story of a chronic drink-related condition. Most of the trouble is caused by **A gin**.

Christ, Ma's Carol!
Tiny Tim gets the shock of his life on Christmas Day when he discovers Mrs Cratchit has a first name.

Leak House
As if a long-drawn-out lawsuit wasn't stressful enough, the Jarndyce residence starts to let in water.

Rime and Punishment

Ancient mariner kills old woman with large bird.

Treasure I Land

Jim Hawkins keeps all the booty for himself.

Tristram Handy

The bawdy adventures of a young odd-job man.

Wuthering Eights

Mean and moody gambler Heathcliff loses to a woman at cards and never gets over it.

War and Pace

This epic novel, set in Russia during the Napoleonic era, rattles along at an astonishing speed.

Inside the book:

War & Pace

once upon a time in gloomy Russia, there was a war

and some posh-types bought it.

the end

Modern Works

Animal Far

All animals are equal but some are more distant than others.

A Clockwork Range

A group of cooks are driven to depraved, violent acts when they are forced to use a wind-up oven.

The English Patent

A badly burned Hungarian soldier tells a nurse about his secret former life granting licences to British inventors.

Fahrenheit 45

In Ray Bradbury's dystopian future, all books are banned and firemen are required to collect and slightly singe them.

The Da Vinci Cod

In which we discover that Mary, the mother
of Jesus, was actually a fish.

Fear and Lathing in Las Vegas

Hunter S. Thompson's novel about a journalist and a lawyer who experiment with a variety of recreational woodworking devices.

Fever Itch

An Arsenal fan, who is never out of his football kit, develops an unfortunate allergy to polyester.

Fist Among Equals

Jeffrey Archer's page-turner about the adventurous private lives of a group of Westminster MPs.

For Who, the Bell Tolls

An early adventure for the Time Lord as the Tardis sets down during the Spanish Civil War.

Get Short!

A loan shark moves to LA hoping to find work in the movies but is told he'll need to do something about his height.

The God of Mall Things

The buying habits of a set of twins in India are a powerful metaphor for the effect of large, enclosed shopping areas on all of our lives.

Gory Park

Graphically violent Russian detective story.

Heal, Chemist!

Paulo Coelho's bestseller about a journeying Spaniard's struggle with blisters.

Harry Otter
Young Harry always knew he was different
from other boys...

His Ark Materials

The dæmons manifest themselves two by two in Philip Pullman's fantastical trilogy.

Lady Chatterley's Over

An upper-class woman causes a scandal by donning whites and bowling overarm.

LOL, ta

Middle-aged professor replies to hilarious text message from attractive pubescent girl.

The Mags

In John Fowles' mystical novel, an English teacher escapes his girlfriend by fleeing to a remote Greek island with all his back issues of the *Reader's Digest*.

Miser

Stephen King's thriller about the horror that befalls a parsimonious novelist.

Moon Rake

James Bond foils a dastardly plan to build allotments in space.

The Name of the Roe

Enigmatic novel by Umberto Eco about the quest for fish eggs in fourteenth-century Italy.

Of Ice and Men

A simple-minded farmhand dreams of moving to Alaska and breeding Arctic rabbits.

On Chesil, Bach

A pair of Dorset newlyweds attempt to ease their first-night nerves by listening to the Brandenburg Concertos.

On the Rad

Kerouac goes on a, like, totally awesome road trip.

The Ridges of Madison County

A middle-aged Italian woman discovers that the path to love is a very bumpy ride.

Right-On Rock

Politically correct seaside gangland thriller from Graham Greene.

The Runway Jury

Courtroom thriller from John Grisham about corruption in the airline industry.

A Series of Unfortunate Vents

A fashion disaster befalls the Baudelaire children when Count Olaf puts too many slits in the back of their jackets.

The Silence of the Labs

Experimental novel, focusing on a clinical killer.

Topic of Cancer

This book's subject might have made the author Henry **iller**. (In fact his troubles stem from a minor foot condition he developed in Italy, as he explains in **Topic of Capri Corn**.)

To the Light Hose

A family in the Hebrides forsake heavy woollen stockings in favour of nylons.

Where Angels Fear to Trad

E M Forster conquers his fear of improvised jazz.

The World According to Gap

A New England novelist and his radical mother deal with life's trials and tribulations in an array of casual attire.

Poetry

Believe Me, If All Those Endearing Young Chars
Thomas Moore promises his feelings towards his cleaning ladies will never change.

The Ballad of Reading AOL
Surrey's internet connection was very poor in Oscar Wilde's day.

Daffodil
It doesn't take very much to fire Wordsworth's imagination.

Dig Gin
Seamus Heaney enjoys a drop of the hard stuff.

Do Not Stand at My Grave and Wee

Mary Frye implores us to show a little respect for the dead.

Gob in Market

Christina Rossetti's heartfelt rant against spitting in public places.

The Hunting of the Nark

A bellman, a boots, a bonnet-maker, a barrister, a broker, a billiard-marker, a banker, a butcher, a baker and a beaver embark on an impossible voyage in pursuit of a supergrass.

I

Kipling is in self-referential mode.

Three Non-Fiction Titles

The Bile
One of the most peevish books of all time. Famous for the grim and cheerless **Ark Ages**, and characters such as **Can**, who is more than able to kill his brother, and the treacherous but hilarious **Judas Is A Riot**.

The Go Delusion
In which Richard Dawkins is ordered out of a church and simply refuses to believe it.

Rosemary Conley's Hip and High Diet
Hugely successful weight-loss programme based on salsa dancing and amphetamines.

The Jumbles
Edward Lear goes shopping for sieves, crockery pots and coppery gongs at car boot sales around the country.

La Belle Dame Sans Merc
A beautiful lady callously abandons her expensive car, with tragic results.

Mending All
Robert Frost launches an ambitious restoration project.

Ode to a Night in Gal
John Keats surprises everyone by following 'Ode on a Grecian Urn' with a risqué sex poem.

Over Beach
Seaside holidays are so last year, according to Matthew Arnold.

The Pied Pier of Hamelin
Everyone is mysteriously drawn to the town's black and white jetty.

A Red, Red Roe
Robert Burns extols the virtues of caviar.

The Rod Not Taken
Robert Frost is ill-prepared for a fishing trip.

Sopping by Woods on a Snowy Evening
Frost's little horse does think it queer that he's gone out on such a terrible night without a coat, what with there being no farmhouse near or anything. Look at him, he's soaked through. Tut.

The Waste Lad
T S Eliot's famous elegy to a young refuse collector.

To Amuse
This Burns poem about a wee timorous beastie is sure to raise a chuckle.

Plays and Musicals

Abigail's Arty
While attending a ghastly drinks do, a woman comes to the conclusion that her teenage daughter doesn't know the first thing about science.

Ant Gone
A headstrong girl in ancient Thebes defies the city elders by demanding a proper burial for her pet insect.

As Pecs of Love
Rippling yarn set in the weights room of a gym.

The Car Taker

Harold Pinter's sparse drama about two brothers who take in a joyrider.

Hess

Musical about a love triangle in Nazi Germany in which Hitler and Goering sing the show-stopping 'I Know Him So Well'.

The Iceman Comet

A group of deadbeats in a bar look forward to the arrival of a travelling celestial object.

Lithe Spirit

A man invites an eccentric psychic over for a seance and she conjures up the ghost of his first wife, a gymnast.

The Mouse Rap

The world's longest-running play about hip hop,
and the quietest.

Loo Back in Anger
Ground-breaking drama that rails against the middle-class passion for bidets.

My Fair Lad
Professor Higgins is delighted to discover that a woman *can* be more like a man.

Noses Off
Michael Frayn's clever farce set in the world of provincial rhinoplasty.

Pamalot
Pam Ayres, the Musical.

Rosencrantz and Guildenstern are Dad
Witty comedy in which Ophelia goes doolally and thinks one of Hamlet's childhood pals is her father.

She Stops to Conquer
In Goldsmith's comedy of manners, a wealthy woman tries to attract a husband by standing completely still.

Tones in His Pockets
A film extra ruins a shoot in rural Ireland when his mobile phone keeps going off.

Tree Sisters
Olya, Masha and Irina keep banging on about going to Moscow, where they want to be in some play called *The Cherry Orchard*.

Vita!
Featuring the hit song 'Don't Cry for Me, Virginia Woolf'.

Weeney Todd
The Titchy Barber of Fleet Street.

Wet Side Story
A couple stage a rumble to decide who gets to sleep in the damp patch. Includes the frivolous **I Feel Petty** and the generic love song **Aria**.

Shakespeare

The world's most prolific playwright was also renowned for his hospitality and given the nickname the **Bar of Avon**. He was considered so brainy that his plays could only be staged in the **Lobe Theatre** in London. To this day, his private life is the subject of intense speculation; apparently he wasn't interested in women unless they were bare-headed, although the sole evidence for this theory seems to be his choice of wife, **Anne Hat Away**.

Some of Shakespeare's Best-Loved Plays

All Swell that End… Well!

Helena tricks Bertram into making her pregnant. He is somewhat surprised.

Mac Bet

One stormy night upon the heath, three witches meet and lay odds on a future King of Scotland passing by in an anorak.

A Midsummer Night's Dram

Two pairs of young lovers take a bottle of whisky into the forest and before long are away with the fairies.

O, Hello!

Desdemona isn't expecting Iago to pop round.

Hm. Let?

The tragedy of an insecure tennis umpire.

Famous Shakespearean Quotations

All the world's a sage
Everyone's a smart arse, according to Jacques.

The lady doth po test too much, methinks
Gertrude doesn't like anyone to take too long in the loo.

Now is the winter of our disco tent!
Richard III always likes a boogie, even when on the move with the troops. At one point the battle at Bosworth field where he is eventually slain becomes so heated, he pleads:
My kingdom for a hose!

**Once more unto the beach,
dear friends, once more!**

Henry V only goes to France so that he
can visit the seaside.

Paring is such sweet sorrow

Juliet can hardly bear to watch Romeo
clip his toenails.

**Toe, or not toe.
That is the question**

Hamlet is tormented with indecision
as he wonders whether it's too cold for
flip-flops.

Rome and Juliet

A young Italian girl, tired of her family always arguing with the neighbours, flees to the capital and finds a nice flat with a balcony.

The Winter's Ale

One December night, the King of Sicily sees the statue of his dead wife come to life. He has, however, had several pints.

Other Publications

Aga Magazine

Country cooking for the over-fifties.

Big I Sue

Legal issues.

Daily Port
News from Britain's coastlines; features a lot of shags.

Het
Celebrity magazine, which gets itself worked up into a right state over sweat stains and cellulite. Similar to **Hell**, which gives us an insight into what the daily life of soap actors and minor royals is really like.

Loser
For people addicted to those 'real-life stories'.

National Go Graphic
Extremely earthy shots from around the world.

Prim
For the more demure reader.

Squire
Specialist magazine for male escorts.

Sunday Ties
Contains helpful advice on what gentlemen should wear to church.

Take a Beak
Weekly magazine for bird watchers.

Vanity Far
The only women's magazine that does not have a beauty section.

Woman and Hoe
One of a number of magazines for the female gardener. Other popular titles include **Good Hosekeeping** and **Inside Sap**.

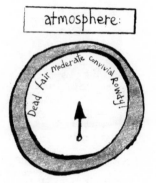

atmosphere:

Dead fair moderate convivial Rowdy!

4. Inventions

From the invention of the **heel**, which changed how early humans moved around, to developments in industry such as Hargreaves' **sinning jenny** – which finally allowed spinsters to have a bit of fun – and Watts' coal-powered sewing machine, the **seam engine**, to the big global family that is the **world wide we**, throughout history, talented and inventive people have striven to make our lives a little bit more convenient.

Many wonderful innovations over the centuries have saved lives, energy, money and time, none more so than that epitome of usefulness, the invention against which all other inventions are measured – the loaf that chews itself, **liced bread**.

Transport

Thousands of years ago, the indigenous peoples of the Arctic use **a yak** to go hunting, before realising some kind of canoe might be easier.

I Saw Three Ships...

Anal barge
Pleasure craft; doesn't float everyone's boat.

Fright vessel
Goods transportation is not for the faint-hearted.

Oracle
Simple, round boat that has no steering equipment, only divine guidance.

When the first bicycles are invented in the early nineteenth century, the unfortunate noises they emit result in them being deemed unsuitable for women to ride, in particular the **penny farting**.

Traversing rough grassland is no longer a problem when the **moor scooter** is pioneered in the early 1900s.

In the 1930s classically trained actors are used to detect aeroplanes for the first time using a system called **RADA**.

A new type of bus is introduced on to the streets of London in the 1950s. The seating is very cramped, much to the delight of the city's lechers, many of whom miss the **roué master bus** to this day.

Opened in 1994, the **Chanel Tunnel** is by far the most stylish route between England and France.

In 1997 Toyota launches the world's first hybrid Pope Mobile, the **Pius**.

House and Home

The 1950s and sixties were a pioneering period for innovation in the home. Housework was made infinitely more bearable by the invention of the **ashing machine**, which smoked for you while you got on with the laundry. When it all got too much you could have a little cry over the **carpet weeper**. (This would later be replaced by a slimming appliance, the **vacuum leaner**.)

Clock/wok/radio
Wind-up kitchen multi-tasker.

Corn fakes

There's no substitute for a proper breakfast.

Electric haver

Scottish invention that helps men stay smooth while talking utter nonsense.

Lush toilet

For the deluxe bathroom.

Pop-up taster

Counter-top appliance that not only browns bread, it also tells you how delicious it is.

Scotch tap

Bathroom device that is always sticking.

Self-leaning oven
Helpfully shifts itself to one side so that you can scrub round the back.

TV emote control
For use during the demise of soap opera characters, old black-and-white films and programmes about abandoned children and/or puppies.

Upperware
Used to store things on very high shelves.

Wire cat-hanger
For a crumple-free pet.

Zoo lens
For photographing animals at close quarters.

Three
Great Inventors

Christopher Cockerel
Had cause to crow about his
revolutionary air-cushioned vehicle for
the Brighton area, the **Hove craft**.

Marie Cure
Lived up to her name.

The Right Brothers
Upholders of truth; best known for
their magnificent **lying machine**.
They also did some work in aviation,
enabling people who wore hairpieces
to fly thanks to their **fixed-wig
aircraft**.

Medicine

There have been many astonishing achievements in the field of medical science; sadly, however, no cure has yet been found for the **common old**. Gentlemen who are past the age of retirement may find themselves becoming obsessed with DIY. This is known as having an **overactive ladder**, and may make a partner **long-sighed**. Sexual activity can continue well into old age; however, at a certain point, women may become freaked out by **winkles** and need to have a little break, the **men pause**.

Young people who are very athletic may experience **rowing pains**; nearly all teenagers fall out with their families, but **kin problems** are quite normal and usually clear up.

Everyone should be aware of a nasty illness that often strikes at weekends: if you experience a pounding headache, excessive thirst and/or vomiting, you may be suffering from **wine flu**.

Ace maker
Internal device that enables cardiac patients to play tennis.

Adhesive ban age
Simply scoop up those sagging jowls and stick them behind your ears.

Bet blockers
Prescribed for people with a gambling problem.

Latex condo
Allows flexible living arrangements with more than one person.

Micro hips
Silicone implants.

Toot brush
Invented in the days when cocaine was prescribed for many ailments.

Other Inventions

Ball baring

Reducing friction is very useful, but some men can take it too far.

Bar meter

Gauges the atmosphere in your local.

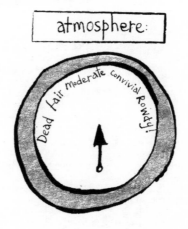

atmosphere

Dead fair moderate convivial Rowdy!

Button hoe
Rather unwieldy device for doing up a coat.

Computer moue
The little pout you do when you get an on-screen error message. Almost as annoying as those **poxy servers**, which are enough to make your **USB memory sick**.

Credit cads
Damn those bankers.

Fat-screen TV
It's true what they say about television adding extra pounds.

Miner slap
Humphry Davy was the first to introduce a wallop round the face as a method of keeping colliers alert.

Ouch-screen phones
All that tapping can take its toll on the fingertips.

Communication

Developed in the 1830s, **Morse ode** was a clever way of sneaking poems past the enemy.

The **gram phone** dates back to the 1880s; you could ring and find out how heavy your records were.

The introduction of a new writing implement, the **all point pen**, in the early twentieth century left people lost for words.

In the 1960s, **touch-toe telephones** allowed us to combine chatting with vigorous exercise.

Small fluorescent reminders not to send love letters to your ex, your boss or random celebrities, **post-it nots** were patented in the 1970s.

Developed in the late 1980s, **nose-cancelling headphones** cleverly minimise and flatter an oversized conk.

Enormous strides in global communication have been made since we entered the internet age. It's easy to keep in touch with friends and relations in South Africa via **Facebook**; those who are prone to nervous laughter can talk to the similarly afflicted on **Titter**. Fancy a burrito or some nachos? **Tex messaging** is a really quick way of ordering via your mobile phone. Or you might prefer a **wifi hotpot**.

For the first thirty or so years of personal computing, **foppy disk drives** were fine and dandy; it did take a long time for CD drives to supersede them, but then **ROM** wasn't built in a day.

Did you know?
The internet search engine was invented in the Yorkshire town of **Goole**.

5. Music

When rock and roll burst on to the popular music scene in the 1950s, Bill Haley's **Rock Around the Cock** caused outrage as for the first time overt references were made in song to farm animals. **Baby Let's Lay House** and **How High the Moo** followed soon after. Then there was Elvis, who scandalised mothers with his awful table manners, in particular **swivelling his HP**. There were many female artists around at the time too: music lovers enjoyed the magic of **Wand Jackson**, the polish of **Rub Murray**, the albumens of **Eggy Lee**, and were very glad when **ETA James** finally arrived on the scene.

Three Fifties Crooners

Bin Crosby
Rubbish.

Bobby Darn
Never had a hole in his socks.

Matt Mono
Only had one leg.

Fifties Hits

Ears on My Pillow
Little Anthony warned us as early as 1958 about the dangers of too much plastic surgery.

He'll Have Tog
Jim Reeves tells his girlfriend that if she wants a new lover she will need to get a heavier duvet.

I Only Have Yes for You
The Flamingos didn't need too much persuasion.

Iota Woman
Ray Charles's new girlfriend is really, really tiny.

Three Elvis Hits

All Hook Up
Elvis has to have all his clothes altered
due to a morbid fear of zips.

I Forgot to Remember to Forge
It seems the King's counterfeit money
business isn't going too well.

It's No or Never
What Colonel Parker says whenever
Elvis asks for any time off.

Just Waking in the Rain
Johnnie Ray really shouldn't have had those whisky chasers.

Mona Is a…
Nat King Cole just can't bring himself to say it.

This Ole Ouse
Rosemary Clooney takes a nostalgic walk through North Yorkshire.

Wondrous Lace
Billy Fury marvels at the skill involved in doily-making.

You Be Log to Me
Jo Stafford's follow-up single to 'Wooden Heart'.

P eople would often burst into song during the **singing sixties**, probably something to do with the drugs they were all taking. Music had a dirtier, earthier feel than in the previous decade, with artists like **Dust Springfield**, **Smoke Robinson** and **Lesley Ore** topping the hit parade. Women began to be called 'chicks' as **Petula Lark** became a household name.

Sixties Hits

Anyone Who Had a Hart
Cilla Black doesn't much mind who she dates, as long as he's a deer farmer.

Big Sender
Shirley Bassey makes fulsome use of Royal Mail.

Expresso Bong
Even clean-cut Cliff Richard couldn't resist a quick puff.

Herd It through the Grapevine
Rumours abound that Marvin Gaye has secretly become a goat farmer in Tuscany.

I'm Into Something God
Popular evangelical number from Herman's Hermits.

Jet Aim
Serge Gainsbourg is instructed by Jane Birkin in the art of keeping the toilet seat clean.

Lad All Over
The Dave Clark Five rejoice in their masculinity.

Loop John B
Beach Boys song that never seemed to get to the end.

Make It Easy on Your Elf
Walker Brothers hit that later became Hogwarts' school song.

Sand By Me
Ben E King loves nothing more than a beach holiday.

Save the Last Dane for Me
Anglo-Saxon war anthem.

Say It Loud, I'm Black and I'm Prod
James Brown controversially takes sides in the Northern Ireland conflict.

Silence Is Olden
Bring on the noise.

Thin
A bit of wishful thinking from Aretha Franklin.

A Whiter Shade of Pal
Racist song that makes no sense.

Beatlemania

When the Beatles started out they looked like politicians, with their **MP tops**, but they soon grew long hair and beards and became the **Fab Fur**. (Paul McCartney was obsessed with his hair and would later form the band **Wigs**.)

Their first album **Please Lease Me** could only be borrowed and **Hep!** was considered a little bit fifties; however **Evolver** was a real development, teenagers strongly identifying with the anthem for the acne-ridden, **I'm Only Seeping**. Things got more graphic with **The Hite Album**, which featured explicit tracks such as **While My Guitar Gently Wees** and **I'm So Tied**.

Some Beatles Favourites

Day Tipper
The boys were only ever generous to waiting staff at lunchtime.

I Feel Fin
John Lennon revealed that one of his hobbies was goldfish tickling.

I Saw Her Sanding There
Paul McCartney liked a girl who could handle a power tool.

We Can Wok It Out
The Beatles' obsession with Asian culture started long before they went to India (see also: **I Wanna Hold Your Han**), although they did still enjoy taking holidays in Europe, singing about it on their number one hit **Love Med**.

Sixties Long Players

Aloe Supreme
John Coltrane is a big fan of natural remedies.

Astra Weeks
Van Morrison sings about an old Vauxhall he borrowed for a month.

Clods
Joni Mitchell's earthy second album.

The Doc of the Bay
Before the release of this album, not many people knew that Otis Redding was a qualified medic.

Electric Ladylad
Jimi Hendrix live in Bangkok.

Three
Rolling Stones
Hits

(I Can't Get No) SATS Faction
Mick Jagger wants to campaign for more school tests, but can't find anyone to join him.

Tart Me Up
Keith Richards is in dire need of a makeover.

You Can't Always Get Hat You Want
Even the Stones find it difficult to get their headgear just right.

PE Sounds
The Beach Boys' ever-popular recordings of forward rolls and star jumps.

Ringing It All Back Home
Bob Dylan finally realises he doesn't have to write what he wants to say on pieces of card, he can just pick up the phone.

The seventies was a decade of contrasts. With its innovative use of clever wordplay, **Pun Rock** was unfamiliar (**The Strangers**), argumentative (**Tiff Little Fingers**) and over the top (**Ham 69**), a far cry from the music of mainstream artists who tended to be posh (**Eton John**) and wholesome (**Bran Ferry, Hall & Oats**), a notable exception being the **Litter Band**, who were filthy.

Seventies Hits

American Pi
Don McLean explains that the circumference of a circle is measured slightly differently in the US.

Born to RN
Bruce Springsteen originally planned to go into nursing. Or the navy.

I Eel Love
Many people found Donna Summer's sexy disco hit a little slimy.

The Joke
No one took the Steve Miller Band very seriously.

Long-Hired Lover from Liverpool

Little Jimmy tires of his cute persona, leaves the Osmonds and spends the rest of his days as a gigolo.

No More Teas (Enough Is Enough)

Barbra Streisand [She did that one herself. Ed.] and Donna Summer's duet became an anthem for coffee lovers everywhere.

Perfect Da

Lou Reed had a great relationship with his father.

Stairway to Haven

Humanist version of Led Zeppelin's greatest hit.

Suck in the Middle With You

Stealers Wheel won't let a bit of middle-age spread spoil a hot date.

Three
David Bowie
Tracks

The Jean Gene
Some people are just born with it.

A Lad Insane
A young David completely loses the plot.

Reel, Reel
Bowie's tribute to the Golden Age of Hollywood.

Water, lo!

After a fractious tour of Belgium, ABBA rejoice at the sight of the Ostend ferry.

We've Only Jus Begun

Karen Carpenter is worried her dinner party will be a disaster as the guests are due to arrive any minute and the sauce has barely started to reduce.

Whole Lotta Rosé

AC/DC enjoy a night of wine, women and more wine.

You're So Van

Speculation is still rife as to whether Carly Simon penned this song about Mr Morrison, Mr Halen or Mr Gogh.

Classic Seventies Albums

After the Old Rush
Neil Young makes sure he only goes to the Post Office to collect his royalties once pension day has safely passed.

The Ambler
Kenny Rogers takes a gentle stroll down the middle of the road.

Apes Try
Carole King's seminal monkey endeavour album.

Blood on the Tacks
Bob Dylan has an unfortunate incident while doing a bit of upholstery.

An Arch in the UK

The Sex Pistols rail against British architecture.

Bridge Over Roubled Water

Simon and Garfunkel rake it in after spending years at the top of the Russian charts.

Hat's Going On

Marvin Gaye gives an extremely detailed account of getting ready to leave the house.

Lose to You

Karen Carpenter has to pretend she's rubbish at tennis so that Richard doesn't sulk.

Sicky Fingers

A brave album charting the Rolling Stones' struggles with bulimia.

Songs in the Key of Lie

Stevie Wonder promises he'll call every day to say 'I love you'. Yeah, right.

Um... Ours?

By album number eleven, Fleetwood Mac had run out of ideas for titles.

Wish You Were Her

Pink Floyd don't bother with the old 'It's not you, it's me' line.

The eighties were quite weird. Michael Jackson sang in a warbly, high-pitched voice and made **Triller** the biggest-selling record of all time, and Bon Jovi released a concept album about bathing a chicken, **Slippery Hen Wet**. Greed, speed and excess were the order of the day for artists such as **Racy Chapman**, **Richard Max** and **Salt 'N' Pep**. The decade also saw a higher than average number of stinkers, most of them produced by **Sock, Aitken and Waterman**.

Eighties Hits

Back in Lack
Despite selling millions of albums, AC/DC find themselves in debt again.

Bony and Ivory
Duet about tolerance and acceptance that only works if one of the singers is white and the other very skinny.

Bras in Pocket
Chrissie Hynde always carries some spare foundation garments.

BT out of Hell
Meatloaf is highly dissatisfied with his telephone service provider.

Carless Whisper

George Michael gives adoring fans a hint that he might be green.

Every Little Thing He Does Is Magic

Sting's tribute to Paul Daniels.

Hell

Lionel Richie's date with a blind girl at a pottery class is a total disaster.

Hold Meow

The Thompson Twins try to persuade their cat to be quiet.

How Soon Is No?

The Smiths would like to get the inevitable rejection over with as quickly as possible.

I Should Be So Lucy
Kylie wishes she had a different name.

Louse!
The Human League's song for the
recently dumped.

Master Baster
Stevie Wonder cooks a mean roast
turkey dinner.

Move, Loser!
Phyllis Nelson would like to get
past, please.

Pips of Peace
Paul McCartney calls for the reassuring
Greenwich Time Signal to be piped into
conflict zones.

This Is Radio Cash

The Clash are quite clear about why they want to have their single played on Radio 1.

Toosh

Kajagoogoo aren't too shy to shake theirs.

Madonna was all over the nineties too, making a bid to be the first female 007 with her **Bond Ambition** tour (and giving a bit too much information about the state of her legs in **The Immac Late Collection**). Everyone else tended to play it safe and the decade was characterised by benign and rather flabby efforts from the likes of **Mariah Care**, **Saggy** and **Old Play**. Even Radiohead went for a nice, cosy feel for their chart-topping album **The Beds**.

Three
Madonna
Singles

Into the Grove
In which the Material Girl extols the
joys of fruit-picking.

Lie: A Virgin
Madonna really isn't fooling anyone.

Rue Blue
Madge really wishes she'd never done
that porn film.

Nineties Hits

Alight
Supergrass set the charts on fire.

Back for God
Take That lose Robbie Williams and are born again. One of a spate of Christian songs in the 90s, including Shania Twain's **I'm Gonna Getcha God** and Weezer's tribute to the high priest of rockabilly, **Buddy Holy**.

Be Live
Ironic hit for the queen of mime, Cher.

Bing Boring
The Pet Shop Boys haven't much time for the crooners of the past.

Bump 'n' Grin
R Kelly has a lot of fun on the dodgems.

Constant Caving

k d lang spends every spare moment pursuing her new underground hobby. The outdoor life was a very popular theme at the time; other tracks include **Don't Peak** by No Doubt, Natalie Imbruglia's **Tor**, and **Everybody Huts** by REM.

Ear Thong

Michael Jackson's attire just gets weirder and weirder.

(Everything Id) I Do it for You

Bryan Adams spends a record-breaking sixteen weeks exploring his unconscious psyche.

Fee

Robbie Williams admits to being a rampant capitalist.

Three Nineties Albums

Bring Your Daughter to the Laughter

Iron Maiden find comedy clubs a good way to bond with their kids.

SARS

Infectious album from Simply Red.

Spic

This collection of offensive songs about the Hispanic community was a surprise global hit for the Spice Girls.

Friends in Low Laces
Garth Brooks' pals always seem to be tripping over.

Gene in a Bottle
Who knew that one of Christina Aguilera's hobbies was molecular genetics?

Gonna Make You SWAT
C+C Music Factory is, in fact, a cover for an elite fighting unit.

Love Hack
B-52s number about a randy journalist.

The Millennium Payer
Cliff Richard rakes it in with this perfectly timed hit.

Mmm BP
Those young Hanson boys were easily tempted by a big-money sponsorship deal.

Morning Gory
The Gallagher brothers can't understand why they keep cutting themselves shaving.

My Heat Will Go On
That Celine Dion one is insatiable.

I'm Non-Gel
Dido's hair goes a bit limp.

Pure Shoes
All Saints only really like one kind of shopping.

Return of the Mac

Mark Morrison is ever so pleased to get his raincoat back.

Tub Humping

Whatever turns you on, Chumbawamba.

The noughties were about guitar bands and girls with attitude, male singers all being a bit **Kanye Wet**. Female artists were noisy (**Girls Loud**) and violent (**Duff**, **Lady Gag**). **My Wine House** lived up to her name, knocking back glasses of plonk **Back To Back**.

Noughties Hits

1/10

Paolo Nutini doesn't rate himself very highly.

Three Bands Popular with Fathers

And You Shall Know Us by the Trail of Dad

The Dad Kennedys

The Grateful Dad

Bonker

Dizzee Rascal is a real hit with the ladies.

Chop Sue

Hard-rock outfit System of a Down want a new host for *A Question of Sport*.

DG Days Are Over

When Florence + the Machine hear how much BBC executives are getting paid, they demand that the Director-General resign.

Everybody's Hanging

A suicidally depressing number from Keane.

Hum 'A'

The Killers need a bit of help finding the right note before they start.

Three Noughties Albums

Intensive Car
Robbie Williams is a boy racer at heart.

On Key Business
The Black Eyed Peas take their music very seriously indeed.

XY
Coldplay took a bold step in recording an album of songs about the human gender determination system.

I Dreamed a Dram
Susan Boyle is Scottish through and through.

Not Far
Lily Allen's follow-up to **Mile**.

The Limb
The campaign to make *X Factor* winner Joe McElderry's song the Christmas Number One cost an arm and a leg. It was a battle of old-style rock versus manufactured pop: **Age Against the Machine**.

Mazing
One of George Michael's favourite pastimes involves visiting a lot of public parks.

Milk Sake
Kelis invents a disgusting new type of rice wine.

Three from
the Kaiser Chiefs

Every Day I Love You
Les and Les
The band express growing admiration for their comedy heroes Dawson and Dennis.

I Predict a Rot
The Chiefs are pessimistic about their pending house survey.

Never Miss a Bet
They're always down the bookies, those boys.

Quick Sad

La Roux is never happy for long.

Reedy

Little Boots is the one with the thin, high-pitched voice.

Rounds for Divorce

Marriage is a lot like a boxing match, according to Elbow.

Sex on Fir

Alfresco fun with Kings of Leon.

She Bans

Ricky Martin's tribute to Mary Whitehouse.

Sine

Take That try to shake their pretty-boy image with a song about the ratio of the side of a triangle to the hypotenuse.

Sinning Around
Kylie went a bit trampy in the noughties.

Tan
Eminem is man enough to admit to using bronzer.

That's My Gal
Shayne Ward is the first X Factor winner to release a cockney song as a single.

Classical Music, Opera and Ballet

Aid
An Ethiopian princess who has been sold into slavery appeals to the international community for assistance.

Anon in D

Pachelbel never owned up to this Baroque favourite.

Argo

In Handel's version of the Greek legend, Jason's voyage to find the Golden Fleece proceeds very slowly indeed.

Candid

Voltaire's novel transformed into an extremely frank opera.

Cos Fan Tutti

As eating salad becomes all the rage in the eighteenth century, Mozart advocates lettuce for all.

Do Carlos!

In Verdi's dramatic opera, Philip II of Spain is urged to do impressions of his family.

For Tuna
Carl Orff devotes part of his masterwork
Carmina Burana to his favourite sandwich
filling.

Fun Era March
Chopin believes that death shouldn't be
all doom and gloom.

The Magic Flue
A prince is led to his true love by an enchanted
chimney.

Night on a Bar Mountain
A group of Russian witches gather for
satanic revelry and some vodka shots.

The Nutcracker Suit
Tchaikovsky's favourite trousers shrink in the
wash.

Three Composers and Three Conductors

Bah!
Bad-tempered music.

List
Supermarket music.

Rave
Music to drive you wild.

_____

Colin Avis
Conductor for hire. Very useful for **Hols**.

Zubin Meta
On a higher plane than the rest.

I'm on Rattle
Always demands to play in the
percussion section.

O hen, grin!

Wagner spends several hours encouraging a chicken to cheer up.

Peter and He-Wolf

A young Russian boy rescues a duck who's been swallowed by a nasty comic-book villain.

Pom and Circumstance

This series of marches by the English composer Elgar was a gift to the Australian people, and includes his famous kangaroo song **Land of Hop and Glory**.

Rid of the Valkyries

In one of the most famous pieces from Wagner's *Ring Cycle*, we finally say goodbye to Brunhilde and her sisters.

To red, or song?
Bizet has the afternoon off and doesn't
know whether to spend it drinking wine
or writing a new tune.

The Tout
Tickets for this Schubert quintet can
only be bought at vastly inflated prices
outside the venue.

Tristan and I Sold
Wagner's tragic tale of a knight and a princess
forced by circumstances to open up a harp shop.

Wan Lake
Ballet in which all the dancers look a
bit peaky.

6. Film

As the silent movie era came to an end, the first 'talking picture', in 1927, came as a huge shock to cinema goers, mainly because the film kept catching fire. Thankfully things have improved since **The Jazz Singe** and we now have a rich legacy of cinematic work with many iconic moments – for example: Humphrey Bogart declaring his love for the golf course:

We'll always have pars,

a sentiment which would be echoed decades later by Han Solo:

May the fore be with you;

Bette Davis finding consolation in cigarettes:

**Don't let's ask for the moon.
We have the tars;**

Clark Gable's unforgettable scorn for flooding in
the Netherlands:

**Frankly, my dear,
I don't give a dam!;**

and Marlon Brando igniting the debate about
recycling:

**I'm gonna make him an offer
he can't re-use**

Abe

Cute pig becomes president of the USA.

9½ Eeks

Mickey Rourke's suggestions for a cosy night in cause considerable alarm.

Aging Bull

A boxer forgets what he came into the ring for.

All the Resident's Men

Two journalists uncover a plot to break into a sheltered housing complex.

Apocalypse, Ow!

A painful journey into the heart of darkness. Famous for the scene in which Lt. Col. Kilgore yearns to be on a tropical island: 'I love the smell of **a palm** in the morning.'

Around the World in 8 Days

An English aristocrat and his butler take a long-haul mini-break.

Three Seventies Blockbusters

Close Encounters of the Hird Kind

Ground-breaking sci-fi version of the TV hymn request show *Praise Be!*

Jaw

A set of killer dentures is on the loose on Amity Island. The only available weapon is some table tennis equipment, prompting Roy Scheider to declare **We're gonna need a bigger bat.**

Tar Wars

In a galaxy far, far away an epic struggle between good and evil rages among rival road builders.

Bell du Jour

A bored Parisian housewife becomes interested in campanology.

Brie Encounter

In the austere war years, a married woman harbours a forbidden passion for French cheese.

Carface

A *screen* test *indicated* that Al Pacino's *hooded* eyes, not to mention his *drive* and his *trunks*, *boots* and other gear made him the *automatic* choice to play *wheeler*-dealer Tony Montana. [The author apologises: Ed.]

Carry On Amping

The most electrifying of the *Carry On* films. Famous for Barbara Windsor getting her woofers out.

Three Bond Films

For You, Eyes Only
James Bond takes an uncharacteristic
vow of celibacy.

The Man with the Olden Gun
Scaramanga would have been a much
better villain if he hadn't been using
a Colt 45.

Tomorrow? Never, Des!
Pierce Brosnan stars as an ageing
crooner who can't get himself
a booking.

The Empire Trikes Back

Luke Skywalker is forced to flee Darth Vader on a small three-wheeled bicycle.

The Even-Year Itch

A married man is tempted by his sultry blonde neighbour, but only when the year is divisible by two.

A Few God Men

'You can't handle the truth!' roars Jack Nicholson's Jesus at Doubting Thomas (played by a serene **Om Cruise**.)

Fight Cub

Brad Pitt and Ed Norton engage in secret *bear-*knuckle fighting.

Forrest Gum

Life is like a box of chocolates, only chewier.

Three Documentaries

Bowing for Columbine
Michael Moore's documentary is the first to link gun crime with excessive politeness.

An Inconvenient Ruth
Al Gore's shocking film reveals that global warming can be traced back to a woman in Biblical times.

No Direction Hom
Martin Scorsese uses archive footage and interviews to profile the intriguing and influential Chinese chef Ken Hom.

Gorgy Girl
Lynn Redgrave ate all the pies.

He Wore a Yellow Ribbon
Pioneering gay western.

The Hustle
Paul Newman risks everything to become the
best seventies disco line-dancer in the country.

Ilk
Film about men who are 'like that'.

In the Loo
Too much information about
politicians at Westminster.

Irates of the Caribbean
In which everyone in the cast gets fed up with
Orlando Boom thinking he's such a big noise.

Three Animated Films

Dumb
The adventures of a really
stupid elephant.

Finding Emo
Cute, lost fish becomes a fan of
emotionally-charged punk rock.

Toy Tory
'To the right of centre, and beyond!'

Jurassic Par

A group of oldies go on a golfing weekend.

Kind Hearts and Cornets

In a musical tour de force, Alec Guinness plays all the members of a brass band.

Lash Dance

Despite being a busy welder, Jennifer Beals finds time to take eyelid batting to a professional level.

Last Tang in Paris

Bittersweet romance.

Life of Bran

Monty Python's satire still upsets many cereal lovers, even though most of them have never actually seen it.

The Lob
American horror film in which Steve McQueen terrorises a small town with a killer tennis shot.

Moon Truck
Cher in an Oscar-winning role as a late-night delivery driver.

Mrs Henderson Resents
Dame Judi Dench is a bit sullen about being cast opposite TV talent show popster Will Young.

Oman Holiday
Audrey Hepburn finds romance with a suave sheikh.

One With the Wind
As the American Civil War rages, a Southern belle has problems with her digestive system.

Three
Horror Films

28 Days Late
Teen pregnancy nightmare.

Rosemary's Bay
A woman moves into a new
apartment block with her husband
and finds herself mysteriously
compelled to grow herbs.

The Blair Itch Project
Gordon Brown's wait to take over
as prime minster becomes
unbearably tense.

Monk E-business

Marx Brothers film set in a monastery where
the monks' commercial savvy is way ahead
of its time.

Paper Moo
A travelling con man forms an unlikely
bond with an orphaned cow.

Petty in Pink
American teenagers squabble over trivial
matters. (One of several eighties films featuring
women who took their tops off a lot and became
known as the **Bra Pack**.)

Plane of the Apes
Goodness, those monkeys were smart.

Pup Fiction
The tale of two violent young dogs
who love cheeseburgers. Bruce Willis
plays a boxer.

Rain Spotting
Film about the weather in Edinburgh.

Three Should-Have-Been Horror Films

Don't Look, NO!
A film so terrifying it commands you not to watch it.

Fatal: A Traction
Glenn Close runs amok with a steam engine.

Hell Dolly!
Musical about a demonic matchmaker.

Rand Hotel

1930s film set in South Africa. Noted for the amazing costumes of **Greta Garb**, who was famously fussy about appearing on the New Year Honours list: **I want OBE alone.**

Reel Without a Cause

A totally pointless film.

Sandal

It turns out John Profumo was also a foot fetishist.

Sleepless in Settle

Romantic comedy set in the Yorkshire Dales.

Some Like it Ho

Two musicians witness a murder and have to flee the Mob by disguising themselves as prostitutes. (**Jack Lemon** is the idiotic one, **Toy Curtis** the flirtatious one.)

GRRrr-

Shat
This film about a womanising private
eye was the first to have someone with irritable
bowel syndrome in the lead role.

Tax Driver

Robert De Niro plays a disillusioned Vietnam vet who gets a job with the Inland Revenue.

They Shoo Horses, Don't They?

While taking part in a dance marathon, a depressed actress demands to be chased.

Trading Laces

Eddie Murphy and Dan Aykroyd swap shoes, with hilarious consequences.

Whisk Galore

The residents of a remote Scottish island can't believe their luck when a ship runs aground and discharges its cargo of 50,000 egg beaters.

Wigs of Desire

In Wim Wenders' German classic, two angels roam Berlin replacing unconvincing toupees.

'And the Scar™ Goes to…'

Every year, Hollywood honours those individuals who have made an indelible mark on the film world and will leave a lasting imprint:

Best Supporting Actor – **Bra Pitt**

Worst Actor – **Bad Pitt**

Most Awesome Performance – **Rad Pitt**

Deepest Performance – **Brad Pit**

Best Supporting Actress – **Ally Field**

Worst Actress – **Bette Idler**

Best Cameo Appearance – **Sharon's Toe**

Best Stand-in – **Johnny Dep**

Most Expensive Actor – **Kevin Coster**

Most Expensive Actress – **Meryl Steep**

Worst Performance in a Musical – **Meryl Strep**

Best Performance in a Musical – **Kim, a Singer**

Best Actor in a Porn Film – **Clit Eastwood**

Best Actress in a Porn Film – **Hilary Wank**

Most Solid Performance – **Jeff Bridge** (also nominated: **Wood Harrelson**)

Most Idiotic Performance – **George Looney** (also nominated: **Warren Batty**)

Most Self-Centred Performance – **Russell Crow** (also nominated: **Me Gibson**)

Person Least Likely to Win – **Glenn Lose** (also nominated: **Reese Wither Soon**)

Musicals

Ain't Your Wagon

A farmer and a gold prospector share a wife, but can't decide who owns the caravan.

Airspray

Racial tensions among high-school students in Baltimore are dispelled with some air-freshener.

Anchors Weigh

Gene Kelly and Frank Sinatra discover that life on the ocean wave requires some heavy lifting.

Aster Parade

Love blooms for Judy Garland and Fred Astaire at a specialist flower show.

The Boy Fiend
Flapper Polly Browne's new beau turns out to be a brute. Starring **Wiggy**, the famous sixties hair model.

Call Me Adam
1950s prequel to *All About Eve*.

Even Brides for Seven Brothers
Six ladies draw lots for a husband and try not to pull the shortest one.

Olive!
Musical based on the life of the evil Popeye's long-suffering, kind-hearted girlfriend.

On the Tow
A navy ship heading for New York with Gene Kelly, Frank Sinatra and Jules Munshin on board breaks down en route.

The Red Hoes

Moira Shearer dreams of becoming a gardener.

Show Bot

Howard Keel scandalises passengers on board a floating cabaret when his trousers fall down during the opening number.

There's No Business Like Sow Business

Ethel Merman enthusiastically takes up pig farming.

7. Miscellany

Sport and Leisure

Some sports require highly specialised skills, equipment or small mammals – the annual Oxford and Cambridge **bat race**, for instance, or **sum wrestling**, which there's no point attempting without a maths degree.

I say, slow down Tarquin!

However, football is a very accessible sport: Premiership side Liverpool only need **a field** to play in, and Charlton Athletic manage in **the alley**. Another popular sport that anyone can take part in is **water poo**. More and more children are taking it up – you'll often hear dads saying they need to 'drop the kids off at the pool'.

With sport comes drama: fans love to see cricketers making a right balls of it – **goolies** – or a footballer being rewarded for a brilliantly clever foul with a **red car**. However, with drama comes danger: a batsman could fall in to the **sumps**, and there's a reason why there's a rugby position called **lose head prop**.

In recent years, many sports have, unfortunately, been blighted by **rug scandals**, when players have been caught keeping their knees artificially warm. But such unfortunate incidents cannot diminish the appeal of big global events like the **World Dart Championship**, in which very unfit men do a two-metre dash; the **Word Cup**, which challenges footballers to string a sentence together; and the Summer and Winter Olympics, which host a vast range of competitive events:

Curing
Two teams push a large ham along a sheet of ice.

Hokey
Contestants put their left leg in but must not take it out again.

Hooting
Athletes compete to see who can laugh the loudest.

Log jump
Field event.

Olé vault

Jumping sport reserved for Spanish-speaking countries.

Quash

The loser gets well and truly annihilated.

Snow barding

Competitors must recite passages from Shakespeare while careering down a slope.

Three Songs
for Golfers

Smells Like Tee Spirit

The Trail of the Lonesome Pin

You Hook Me All Night Long

Three Songs for
Fishing Enthusiasts

Hake, Rattle and Roll

The Long and Winding Rod

Mr Bo Angles

Sow jumping

Just getting the pig on to the horse is a challenge.

Tale tennis

Two people bat stories back and forth and try not to miss the point.

Tripe jump

This notoriously difficult event requires athletes to clear a cow's stomach in three bounds. Not to be confused with the **hop, kip and jump**, where contestants have a little snooze at the halfway point.

Wightlifting

Strong men try to lift an entire island. [Jerks. Ed.]

For those looking to take up a new leisure activity, **waking** is a good way to start the day and much less strenuous than jogging. Once you've mastered that, you might progress to **ambling**, and eventually take up **landscape panting**, where you try to get gently out of breath in a picturesque environment. If the aim is to lose a few pounds, that can be done at a **hopping centre**.

Arts and rafts are excellent pursuits for those of a buoyant nature. **Basket waving** is very good for the upper arms; **cross-titch** – annoying a very small person by poking them with a needle – is a most satisfying pastime, as is **nitting**, where two needles are used to remove nasty parasites. Music is a wonderful hobby, although **paying the piano** can be an expensive business. A cheaper option, provided you have a chimney, is to **play the flue**.

Home improvement is another popular way of spending leisure time: **home eco-rating** can make your house much more environmentally friendly, and **double lazing** is a great way of conserving energy. Those who are anxious about their DIY abilities could start by building some **new selves**, while any pent-up anger can be released by decking the garden or **axing the car**.

Toys and Games

Acton Man
Aimed at young boys who want to live in west London when they grow up.

Etch A Ketch
Mechanical drawing board for drawing two-masted sailing boats.

Gran Theft Auto

Controversial video game in which pensioners commit criminal acts.

Indy

A doll for girls who don't like the more mainstream Barbie.

Lime

A very simple toy, consisting of a can of bright green.

Rayons

The first man-made, easy-care wax drawing sticks.

Snakes and Adders

Ancient Egyptian board game. Cleopatra was playing shortly before her death.

Space Hoper

Owned by every child who ever wanted to be an astronaut.

Tickle Me ELO

Hugely popular interactive doll version of the high-voiced, woolly-haired rocker Jeff Lynne.

Tin Solders

Junior metalworking kit.

Toll Dolls

Collectable fluorescent-haired piggy banks.

Top Rumps

Despite the popularity of video and internet games, teenage boys still seem very happy with these old-fashioned picture cards.

Trivial PR Suit

The winner is the first to get six minor celebrities involved in pointless litigation.

Wii FT

Popular video game for exercising your stock-market trading skills at home.

Three Card Games

Five-Cad Stud
Played by dishonourable scoundrels.

Three-Card Bra
A simple version of Strip Poker.

Wist
Ahh… I used to love playing that.

Days of National Importance

Eater Sunday
National Chocoholics Day

Ban Holiday Monday
National Workaholics Day

Shove Tuesday
National Batter Day

Sh! Wednesday
National Library Day

Mandy Thursday
National Barry Manilow Day

Goo Friday
National Porridge Day

Hoy Saturday
National Orkneys Day

Fashion

1930s

Animal-print fabrics arrive from America and are made into jazzy **zoo suits**.

Gentlemen wishing to prove their animal magnetism wear **double-beasted** suits.

1940s

During the Second World War people have to wear items of utility clothing: these become the first **ready-to-war** collections.

Later, British women adopt the Parisian model of carrying small dogs around, known as **pet-à-porter**.

1950s

Men who want to look like Elvis but can't afford expensive pomade **lick back** their hair.

Ladies' **wing coats** really take off.

1960s

Coco Chanel's **weed suits** prove a big hit with the counter-culture.

Campaign groups spring up in opposition to a severe new haircut under the slogan **Ban the Bob**.

Three Songs for Animal Lovers

Cat, Speak French!

The Sow Must Go On

Up Panda Way

Three Great Artworks

The Cream
Edvard Munch's single best work.

Tarry, Night
Van Gogh was not really a morning person (although he did later paint **I Rise**.)

The Tinker
Rodin's iconic sculpture of a kettle-mender.

1970s

Some women miss out on the feminist revolution and are stuck in the kitchen with their **hot pans**.

Hippies favour clothes made with natural materials – **log dresses** become all the rage.

1980s

Yuppies who work in the City like to show off their **sell suits**.

Princess Diana cultivates a well-bred look with her **filly blouses**.

1990s

The decade of the **gunge** look: the style is fluid and very messy.

Chocoholics hold their hair back with **crunchies**.

2000s

Musicians who use a lot of heavy bass start a trend for **low-sung jeans**.

Many employers try to smarten up their workplaces by having staff dress as university professors once a week on **dress-don Friday**.

Celebrity Chefs and Their Specialities

Comfort Food:
Hug Fearnley-Whittingstall

Dog Food:
Pal Rankin

Flamboyant Dishes:
Gay Rhodes

Mediterranean Dishes:
Jamie Olive

Merchandising:
Rick's Tin

Slow Cooking:
Nigel Later

Soufflés:
The Airy Bikers

Food

British cuisine has never had a particularly good reputation, perhaps dating back to the post-war period of the 1940s and fifties when **food ratios** meant that exactly two pieces of lard had to be eaten for every one lump of suet. People were generally delighted when they came to an end, although many did miss the instant energy boost that came from **powered egg**. In the 1960s, dinner parties were a chance to show off new culinary creations: you might be served **pawn cocktail**, a clever board game and starter in one, on a table made of **teak Diane**. Any undesirable guests could be filtered out using a **sod siphon**.

Dining in England has historically been a solitary affair, except at weekends when there's the **Sunday join**. The Scots reportedly have one of the unhealthiest diets in Europe, which is surprising as they **lack pudding**. However they do make up for this once a year, on **Buns Night**. Wales's national dish has to be kosher, as prescribed by the **Welsh Rabbi**, and in Ireland everyone is very thin because rather than eat, the **Irish sew**.

Cookery programmes have been a staple ingredient of our television diet for some time now. Delia Smith is famous for her **Complete Cookery Curse**, where all she has to do is

Three Popular Desserts

Fruit Rumble
Good for scraps.

Ice Cram
Good for stuffing yourself.

Lemon Tote
Good for carrying around.

mention an ingredient and it immediately sells out. Current popular cookery programmes include **Come Die with Me**, the search for a killer amateur chef and **Master Che**, the search for the most revolutionary.

Places

For both economic and environmental reasons, more and more of us are choosing to spend our holidays in the UK, and British towns and cities have much to recommend them. For a good breakfast head for the **Brecon Bacons** but if you fancy a swim give **Wan Sea** a miss, and don't bother with **Lack Pool** either. Teesside is a lovely part of the country, but stay on the outskirts because the **middle's rough**. By all means pay a visit to Northern Ireland's capital city but **be fast**, then head straight to **a trim** for a haircut. For a livelier pace try **Presto**, or **Pert**: a visit there is always an uplifting experience.

Tourist Attractions

Alto Towers
Where the attractions are deep-voiced female singers.

Bling Broke Castle
Rather too many heavy crown jewels were housed here.

Buckingham Place
The global economic crisis has even forced the royal family to downsize.

Caring Cross
London's biggest nursing station.

Chat Worth
This Peak District stately home is really something to talk about.

The Den Project
EastEnders theme park (built circa 1985).

Egoland
The place to go when you need to give your self-esteem a boost.

Flaming Land
Watch out, those birds are fiery.

The London Ee!
It's really scary up there.

Long Let House
Come to Somerset and stay for as long as you like.

Money World
Costs an absolute fortune to get in.

Three British Bridges

Lift-On Suspension Bridge
The only bridge in the world to use a
system of pulleys.

Sever Bridge
Cuts Wales off from England.

Umber Bridge
Painted a lovely dark orange.

The Norfolk B-Road

OK, so Norfolk doesn't have that many
attractions. It's a really nice road,
though.

The North York Moos

Big dairy farming area.

The Pea District

The home of the Jolly Green Giant.

The Pembrokeshire Coat

A set of **National Tails**.

Three European Gems

Bilbo
Spanish city devoted to Tolkien's Hobbit.

Rotter, Da!
Dutch city renowned for its cheeky children.

V. Nice
Really lovely Italian city.

Stateside

Alt Lake City
They do things differently there.

August
Georgia is full of fine, upstanding folk.

Florid
So hot you're liable to go very red in the face.

Main
Principal state of New England.

Miss Uri
State that suffers from a lack of spoon benders.

Sacrament

Extremely religious town in California.

Washing On

The cleanest state in the Northwest.

Around the World

Bag Dad

Where single women go in pursuit of the older gentleman.

Be Liz

Every person in this Central American country is named after the queen.

Bog, ta?

It's not easy to find a toilet in the Colombian capital.

Bruni
Madame Sarkozy has her own oil-producing state.

Buenos Airs
A bit up itself.

Cape of Good Hop
Home of the finest beers.

Cub
Relatively young Communist state.

The Gob Desert
The loudest place on earth.

Helman Province
Where mayonnaise comes from.

I Bet

Gambling capital of the Far East.

Lags

Not quite up there with other Nigerian cities.

Ma Law

In this part of Africa whatever your mother says goes.

Mink

Belarus is renowned for its fur coats.

Napes

Italian neck of the woods.

St Peter's Bug

Will have you *Russian* to the toilet. (Groan. Ed.)

Tong
Where curly hair originated.

U Wait
Service isn't exactly speedy in the Gulf.

VAT Can City
Everything is tax-free here, except soft drinks.

Three Countries to Avoid

Hungry

Pain

No Way

Acknowledgements

This book would never have happened without the intelligent, funny (and, I'm sure, extremely good-looking) folk of Twitter. Thanks so much to everyone who joined in and passed it on. Without Steve Bowbrick and Jem Stone of the Radio 4 blog, #radio4minus1letter would never have been seen in the BBC staff magazine *Ariel* by Paddy O'Connell, Rupert Allman and the team at Broadcasting House, and therefore never been heard by the author Tim Binding, who laughed so much he tracked me down and suggested I expand the idea into a book. He also gave me the title. I'm grateful to them all and to Tom McLaughlin for his wonderful illustrations, and for taking a chance.

My agent Tom Williams and Louisa Joyner and Sophia Brown at Virgin Books made the whole thing happen and have provided guidance and encouragement throughout. I'd also like to thank John Andrew, Jonathan Dryden Taylor, Denis Harley, Anke Lueddecke, Eileen McKue, Jud Mulholland, Alan Smith and Mark Simpson for offering invaluable suggestions and advice; Emma Bloxham, Dermot Finch, Daniel Frankl, Zoë Gilmour, Christine Hayes, Steve Lambley, Drew Leckie, Fintan McDonagh and my BBC colleagues for their interest and excitement; and my parents, Pat and Archie McGregor, for their calm acceptance of yet another hair-brained scheme.